Production Num : 00087331
Order Number : N0203595-00
Page Number   : 16
Date   : 08 /16 /99
Time   : 08:51:38 am

641.
5944
Fis

C.1

Fisher, Teresa.

A flavor of France

DATE DUE	BORROWER'S NAME	ROOM NUMBER
2/6	Jaqueline	10/12/02
214	Maricela	11-7-02
307	Brianda C.	213
	Jennifer Romero	218

641.
5944
Fis

C.1

Fisher, Teresa.

A flavor of France

641.
5944
Fis

Food and Festivals
FRANCE

Teresa Fisher

RAINTREE
STECK-VAUGHN
PUBLISHERS
A Steck-Vaughn Company

Austin, Texas

Food and Festivals

FRANCE

Other titles:

The Caribbean ● China ● India
Mexico ● West Africa

Cover photograph: A market trader in Antibes, selling peppered salami and other cold meats

Title page: A girl and her brother picking bunches of grapes in a vineyard in Provence

Contents page: A float in the Nice Carnival parade

Published by Raintree Steck-Vaughn Publishers, an imprint of Steck-Vaughn Company

Printed in Italy. Bound in the United States.
1 2 3 4 5 6 7 8 9 0 03 02 01 00 99

Library of Congress Cataloging-in-Publication Data
Fisher, Teresa.
A flavor of France / Teresa Fisher.
    p.   cm.—(Food and festivals)
Includes bibliographical references and index.
Summary: Discusses some of the foods enjoyed in France and describes special foods that are part of such specific celebrations as Christmas, Mardi Gras, and Menton's Lemon Festival. Includes recipes.
ISBN 0-8172-5550-8
1. Cookery, French—Juvenile literature.
2. Food habits—France—Juvenile literature.
3. France—Social life and customs—Juvenile literature.
[1. Food habits—France. 2. Cookery, French.
3. France—Social life and customs]
I. Title. II. Series.
TX719.F585 1999
641.5944—dc21   98-15671

CONTENTS

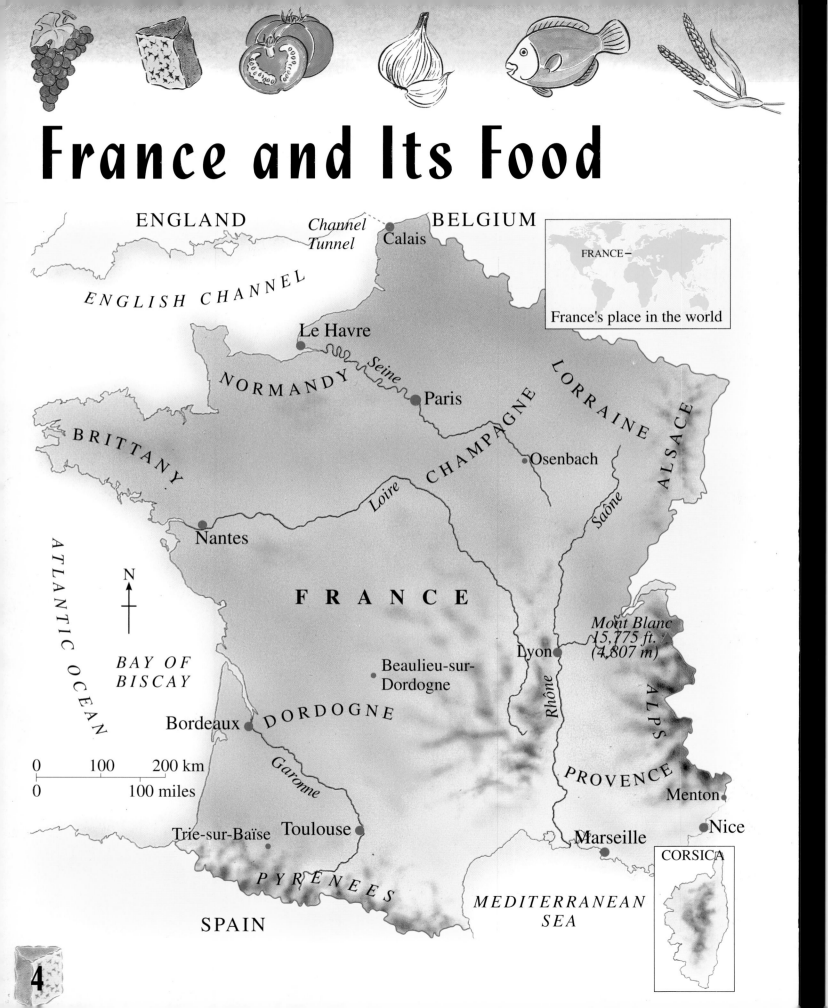

France and Its Food

ENGLAND

Channel Tunnel

Calais

BELGIUM

ENGLISH CHANNEL

FRANCE —

France's place in the world

Le Havre

Seine

NORMANDY

Paris

LORRAINE

CHAMPAGNE

ALSACE

Osenbach

BRITTANY

Loire

Saône

Nantes

ATLANTIC OCEAN

N

F R A N C E

BAY OF BISCAY

Mont Blanc 15,775 ft. (4,807 m)

Lyon

Beaulieu-sur-Dordogne

ALPS

Rhône

DORDOGNE

Bordeaux

0   100   200 km

0   100 miles

Garonne

PROVENCE

Menton

Trie-sur-Baïse   Toulouse

Marseille

Nice

P Y R E N E E S

MEDITERRANEAN SEA

CORSICA

SPAIN

CHEESE

Nearly every region of France produces its own special type of cheese. There are over 365 types in total. Many, such as Brie, Camembert, and Roquefort, are famous all over the world.

WHEAT

Wheat is one of France's largest crops. It is used to make French bread, which is bought freshly baked every day.

FISH

French people eat lots of different fish and seafood, including sole and turbot from the English Channel, shellfish from Brittany, and sardines from the Mediterranean.

VEGETABLES

Many different vegetables are grown throughout France. Onions, shallots, and garlic are essential in French cooking. They add a strong flavor to many dishes.

FRUIT

The most important fruits are apples to produce cider and grapes to produce France's famous wines. Apricots, cherries, strawberries, melons, peaches, oranges, lemons, plums, and pears are also favorites.

OLIVES

Black and green olives grow in southern France, during the long, Mediterranean summers. Many are crushed to make olive oil, which is used for cooking.

5

Food and Farming

France is the largest country in Western Europe. It is famous for its fashion, perfume, fine wines, and its *haute cuisine* (high-quality cooking). French dishes are always prepared with the freshest, tastiest ingredients available. Lots of garlic, herbs, and spices bring out the flavors.

FROGS AND SNAILS

In France frogs' legs are a delicacy. They taste surprisingly like chicken and are delicious served with lots of parsley. Snails are another delicacy, eaten piping hot with butter and garlic.

Frogs' legs don't look very pretty, but once they are cooked, they're delicious.

Well-known dishes include pâté (a paste of mashed meat or fish), *quiche Lorraine* (egg and bacon tart), and *coq au vin* (chicken and wine casserole). A popular fish dish is a soup called *bouillabaisse*. In the mountains, cheese fondue (chunks of bread dipped in hot melted cheese) is always fun to eat.

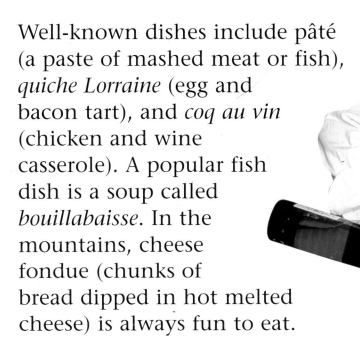

This chef is preparing a traditional soup, called *bouillabaisse*.

Farming

France has more farmland than any other country in Western Europe. This means that French farmers can produce most of the fruit and vegetables, cereals, meat, and dairy products that the country needs. French people do not have to buy much food from abroad.

A grape harvest in a vineyard near Bordeaux

▲ Villagers in Provence gather in an olive grove before their olive festival.

Different crops grow best in different regions. In the south, where the climate is warmer, the region of Provence is well-known for its olives, tomatoes, fish, herbs, and citrus fruits. Western France, which has more rain, is known for its fruit and vegetables.

▲ Black and green olives make an appealing snack.

Cheese and Dairy Products

In northern France, the fertile pastures are ideal for grazing cows. Normandy is famous for its dairy products, such as milk, cream, and cheese. France produces enough types of cheese for a person to eat a different one every day of the year. Many places even hold special cheese festivals.

Livarot cheese is one of France's oldest cheeses. It is soft and creamy, with a reddish-brown rind and a strong smell. At the annual Livarot Cheese Festival, the local people wear traditional costumes and there is singing and dancing.

This man is holding a wheel of Brie, which is a soft, creamy cheese.

Markets

The best time to buy local food in France is on market day. Most towns and villages hold their market day in the main square, once or twice a week. Large cities, such as Paris and Marseille, have fruit, vegetable, and fish markets every day.

TRUFFLES

Truffles are a very rare kind of underground mushroom, which are about the size of golf balls. They are highly prized for their flavor. Truffles are sniffed out of the earth by pigs on leashes, then sold for high prices at local markets.

Local farmers sell fresh fruit, flowers, vegetables, meat, eggs and cheese, and special local foods such as walnuts, honey, herbs, and truffles.

▲ Truffle hunting with a pig in the Dordogne

This market trader is ▶ holding peppered salami, which is a favorite French delicacy.

Christmas

Most people in France belong to the Roman Catholic religion. One of their most important festivals is Christmas, the birthday of Jesus Christ.

Christmas celebrations in France begin on December 6 with the Festival of Saint Nicholas, the patron saint of children. You may know Saint Nicholas better as Santa Claus or Father Christmas.

It's fun when Santa Claus comes to town!

In some towns, a man dressed as Saint Nicholas rides through the streets on a donkey and hands out candy and gingerbread cookies to the children.

Christmas Eve

On Christmas Eve, which is on December 24, families get together for a special meal, called *Le Réveillon*. It usually starts with oysters, smoked salmon, or *foie gras* (a delicious duck-liver pâté). The next course may be turkey with chestnut stuffing, roast potatoes, and many different vegetables. The French may serve a fizzy white wine, called champagne, with the meal.

▲ Many different dishes are prepared for the feast of *Le Réveillon*.

If anyone is still hungry, there is the Yule Log, which is a rich chocolate cake in the shape of a log. It is coated in a creamy chocolate, vanilla, or coffee icing. There is a recipe for a yule log on the next page.

PROVENCE DESSERTS

In Provence, for dinner on Christmas Eve, fish is more popular than turkey. But the best part of the meal is the dessert—thirteen different kinds, including dried fruits (raisins, figs, and dates), nuts and nougat, cream cakes, and clementines.

▲ A traditonal Yule Log, with miniature Christmas decorations

Yule Log

EQUIPMENT

Chopping board

3 bowls

Sieve

Wooden spoon

Round-ended knife

Fork

Christmas cake decorations

INGREDIENTS

1$\frac{1}{2}$ oz. (50 g) unsweetened chocolate

2 teaspoons instant coffee

7 Tablespoons (100 g) soft butter

1 cup (200 g) confectioner's sugar

1 roll-shaped sponge cake

1

Break the chocolate into a small bowl. Stand it in a larger bowl, half-full of hot water. Stir until melted. Add the coffee.

2

Put the soft butter in another bowl. Gradually add the sugar through the sieve and beat with the wooden spoon until creamy. Beat in the chocolate and coffee mixture.

3

Put the sponge roll on the chopping board and spread the mixture over it with the knife.

4

Use a fork to make striped marks like bark. Decorate the log with Christmas cake decorations.

Festival of Kings

The *Fête des Rois* (Festival of Kings), on January 6, celebrates the time when three kings visted Jesus and gave him presents of gold, frankincense, and myrrh. In France, this festival is the day when families and friends give Christmas presents to each other.

For dessert on the *Fête des Rois*, a special cake, which contains a lucky charm, is served. If you find the charm in your piece of cake, you become king or queen for the day and wear a crown.

Queen for the day on the *Fête des Rois*!

Mardi Gras

Mardi Gras is carnival time in France. It is an ancient festival celebrated in Catholic countries on Shrove Tuesday, at the end of February or the beginning of March. Shrove Tuesday is the day before Lent begins. In the past, it was forbidden to eat meat or other animal products during Lent. So Mardi Gras was a time to eat up any surplus supplies in the house.

Today, Mardi Gras is always a time of great feasting, with lots of parties and big family meals. Many French towns and cities have magnificent carnival parades.

THE MEANING OF "MARDI GRAS"

The name "Mardi Gras" means "Fat Tuesday" in French. The word "carnival" comes from the Latin words "carne vale," which means "goodbye to meat."

Villagers in traditional costume at a Mardi Gras parade in Alsace

Nice Carnival

The biggest carnival takes place every year
in the city of Nice (pronounced "Neece"), on
the south coast of France. The streets come
alive with brass bands, dancers, fireworks,
and flower battles.

The highlight of the
carnival is always a huge
procession of decorated
floats, carrying people
wearing costumes and
funny masks. They toss
striped hard candy, called
berlingots, into the crowds
from the floats. They even
throw big chunks of nougat,
which is a delicious, chewy
white fudge made locally
from honey and almonds.

A brightly colored
carnival float

Crêpes

Crêpes, or pancakes, are the traditional dish eaten throughout France on Shrove Tuesday. They contain either savory fillings such as cheese, ham, or seafood or sweet fillings such as lemon and sugar, chocolate sauce, or jam. Crêpes are fun to make—especially when you try and toss them! Some towns organize pancake-tossing competitions to see who can toss the most pancakes or who can toss them the highest.

Crêpes

INGREDIENTS
(makes 12 crêpes)

1²/₃ cups (250 g) flour
Pinch of salt
2 eggs
1 cup (¹/₄ l) milk
3 Tablespoons (40 g) melted
  butter
Sugar or jam

EQUIPMENT

Bowl	Whisk
Sieve	Frying pan

1 Sift the flour and salt into a bowl. Add the eggs, milk, and melted butter.

2 Whisk well and leave for an hour.

3 Ask an adult to pour a little of the mixture into a hot, greased frying pan. Cook over a high heat until the underside is golden brown.

4 Toss or turn the crêpe over and cook the other side. Dust the crêpes with sugar or spread with jam. Roll them up and serve.

Ask an adult to cook the crêpe. Don't try tossing the pancake yourself.

19

Easter

Easter is another important religious festival in France. Most families go to church to celebrate the resurrection of Jesus Christ.

Good Friday marks the start of Easter and the end of Lent. Since animal products, including eggs, were forbidden during Lent in the past, some regions of France still celebrate Good Friday by making omelettes with freshly laid eggs.

Lent is celebrated with chocolate eggs as well as real ones. People give and receive chocolate Easter eggs as presents.

Children painting hard-boiled eggs for Easter

A Special Lunch

After church on Easter Sunday, most families celebrate with a big lunch. Everyone, from grandparents to grandchildren, gathers for this special lunch, which may have four or five courses and lasts all afternoon. Most families cook a feast of their favorite dishes, or local specialties, accompanied by lots of potatoes and vegetables.

EASTER-EGG HUNTS

Easter-egg hunts are held on Easter Sunday each year. Children are told that while they are asleep at night, the Easter Bunny hides miniature chocolate and hard-boiled eggs around their homes and yards. In the morning they race to find the most eggs!

Looking for Easter eggs on an Easter-egg hunt

Provence-style lamb kebabs

In mountain areas, roast kid (baby goat) is popular. In Périgord, in western France, many families eat duck. However, the most popular meal at Eastertime is lamb, which is cooked in many different ways. One popular lamb dish from Provence, in southern France, is Provence-style lamb kebabs. The recipe is easy to make and the dish is very good (you can find it on page 23).

Provençe-style Kebabs

INGREDIENTS (serves 4)

1 lb. (¹/₂ kg) lamb, cut into bite-sized cubes
2 Tablespoons olive oil
Pinch of salt & pepper

1 peeled onion, cut into bite-sized pieces
1 green pepper, cut into bite-sized pieces

Thyme, rosemary, and bay leaves
2 tomatoes, quartered

Mix the lamb, oil, salt, pepper, and herbs in a bowl. Leave them for 2 hours, stirring occasionally, so that all the flavors blend together.

Thread the pieces of lamb, tomato, onion and pepper, one after the other, onto the skewers.

Place the kebabs under a hot broiler for 10 minutes, turning regularly.

Serve immediately on a bed of rice, with salad.

Always be careful when using a hot broiler. Ask an adult to help you.

Food Festivals

Most towns and villages in France hold special food festivals, which celebrate their local produce. There are garlic festivals, wine festivals, plum festivals, oyster festivals—even frog festivals!

Beaulieu-sur-Dordogne is famous for growing strawberries. Its Strawberry Fête in May always has many stands where homemade products, such as strawberry jam, are sold. Every year, local people pick as many strawberries as possible and take them to four chefs, who bake an enormous strawberry tart.

GIANT STRAWBERRY TART

One strawberry tart made at the Strawberry Fête in Beaulieu-sur-Dordogne is in the *Guinness Book of Records*. It is the biggest in the world! The tart was made with 1,870 lbs. (850 kg) of strawberries and measured 23 ft. (7 m) across.

This record-breaking strawberry tart is the biggest in the world!

▲ They're off! Snail racing in the Osenbach Snail Festival.

▲ Snails stuffed with parsley and butter, ready to cook

Snail Festival

The highlight of Osenbach's Snail Festival is snail racing. As you know, snails move very, very slowly, so the villagers try to speed them up by holding lettuce leaves in front of them. As the snails race, spectators try to guess which one will go the fastest. In the evening, everyone enjoys a local delicacy—large, edible snails, served hot with runny garlic butter.

Lemon Festival

One of France's most famous food festivals is Menton's Lemon Festival, in February, which lasts for two weeks. Menton is in Provence, in the south of France, where the landscape and climate are ideal for growing oranges and lemons.

The Lemon Festival always attracts thousands of visitors from around France. They watch spectacular parades of floats made of oranges and lemons and eat tangy orange and lemon tarts, jams, and ice cream. In the evenings, it's fun watching the colorful dancing and fireworks displays. Lemon mousse is a favorite dessert around this time. You can find the recipe on page 28.

Women throwing ▶ candy from a moving float, in the Menton Lemon Festival parade

▼ This octopus is made from hundreds of oranges and lemons.

La Jangada

Lemon Delight

INGREDIENTS
(serves 2)

$1/3$ cup (50 g) granulated sugar

$2/3$ cup (150 g) plain yogurt

2 oz. (50 g) cream cheese

$3/4$ cup (150 g) heavy cream

$1/2$ lemon

EQUIPMENT

2 mixing bowls

Lemon squeezer

Rubber spatula

Whisk

2 small dishes

1

Put the sugar and cream cheese in one bowl and mix well. Add a teaspoon of lemon juice, or more, to taste.

2

Put the cream in another bowl and whisk until it forms firm, white peaks. Fold in the yogurt.

3

Add the cream and yogurt mixture to the sugar and cream cheese. Gently fold together.

4

Spoon the mixture into two small dishes. Decorate each dish with a slice of lemon and chill in the refrigerator for two hours.

A delicious bean
cassoulet

Pig-squealing Festival

One of the strangest festivals in France is the Pig-Squealing Championship at Trie-sur-Baïse, in southwest France. At this festival, local farmers and villagers have a big lunch, where all the dishes contain pork. There are simple ham and sausage dishes, as well as more unusual dishes such as black pudding (made with pigs' blood), *cassoulet* (a casserole of duck, bacon, sausage, and beans), and pigs' feet. After lunch, a competition is held to see who can sound most like a pig!

Glossary

Carnival A festival held in February in many countries, just before Lent.

Casserole A dish made with several ingredients, which are cooked for some time in a covered pot so the flavors blend together.

Chef A cook.

Citrus fruits A family of fruits including lemons, oranges, limes, and grapefruit.

Crops Plants that are grown for food, such as wheat, apples, barley, and tomatoes.

Dairy products Milk products, such as butter, cream, and cheese.

Delicacy A type of food that is considered very special and delicious.

Edible Suitable to eat.

Fold If a recipe tells you to "fold" a mixture, gently lift and turn the ingredients repeatedly from the bottom, rather than beating or stirring them.

Floats Platforms on wheels, which are usually highly decorated and used in carnival processions.

Guinness Book of Records A special book listing record-breaking achievements (the biggest, the fastest, the smallest, etc.).

Ingredients All the different foods needed to make a recipe.

Myrrh A substance from certain trees, which is used in perfume and medicine.

Parades Processions of people, often in costume.

Resurrection The moment when Jesus Christ rose from the dead on Easter Day, after dying on the Cross on Good Friday.

Rind The skin or peel of fruit.

Roman Catholic A member of the Roman Catholic Church, which is headed by the Pope, in the city of Rome.

Savory Spicy or salty as opposed to sweet.

Shallots Small purple onions.

Shrove Tuesday The day before Lent begins. In France this day is called *Mardi Gras*.

Books to Read

Denny, Roz. *A Taste of France* (Food Around the World). Austin, TX: Raintree Steck-Vaughn, 1994.

Fisher, Teresa. *France* (Country Insights). Austin, TX: Raintree Steck-Vaughn, 1997.

Loewen, Nancy. *Food in France* (International Food Library). Vero Beach, FL: Rourke Publications, 1991.

McKay, Susan. *France* (Festivals of the World). Milwaukee, WI: Gareth Stevens, Inc., 1998.

Waldee, Lynne Marie. *Cooking the French Way* (Easy Menu Ethnic Cookbooks). Minneapolis, MN: Lerner Publications, 1982.

Photograph and artwork acknowledgments

The publishers would like to thank the following for contributing to the pictures in this book:

Ace 12; Anthony Blake 18, 22; Cephas 7, 8, 9 (top), 9 (bottom), 11 (top), 13 (top), 13 (bottom), 25, 29; Chapel Studios 21; Eye Ubiquitous 5; Getty Images *Title page*, 27; Image Bank 10; Robert Harding *Cover*, 20, 26; Rex Features 6, 24, 25; Trip 15, 16, 17; Wayland Picture Library 5. Fruit and vegetable artwork is by Tina Barber. Map artwork on page 4 is by Hardlines. Step-by-step recipe artwork is by Judy Stevens.

Index

Page numbers in **bold** mean there is a photograph on the page.